WHERE CHARLES TAYLOR
WENT WRONG

WHERE CHARLES TAYLOR WENT WRONG

A Series of Straight Talks On
Former Liberian President Charles Taylor's
Missteps in Liberia and Sierra Leone

Max Willie

Rev. date: 06/25/2013

To order additional copies of this book, contact:
Xlibris Corporation
1-888-795-4274
www.Xlibris.com
Orders@Xlibris.com
126859

Contents

"Issues surrounding the frantic international efforts to prosecute Charles Taylor for a war in Sierra Leone without regard to a greater consequential civil war conducted in Liberia by Taylor are left for a more conscientious and worthy debate."

"The extent of the surpluses suffered in Liberia, a tiny country of three and a half million people far surpassed what can be endured even by bare minimum human modesty."

"The hope of Liberians were ignited further, Liberians who recognized Taylor as having the wherewithal, as well as the political poise and equanimity to dig the country out of brokenness and impoverishment."

"After years of excruciating struggle against Samuel Doe's regime, and up against the military might of 10 African nations, allied with four Liberian warring groups; having survived all, Taylor saw the country he set out to "liberate" as a private scheme where everything within the border of Liberia belong to him and under his control."

"Domestic dissent was rife over Taylor's blind-eye shown to the basic social needs of the population, and for his implicit endorsement of a culture of impunity in Liberia."

"With his incessant support to Foday Sankor, Taylor became the main article of suspicion and was counted as the chief architect of a war of such magnitude and grave consequence. This scenario, "international bias" aside, offered global actors the Carte blanch or perhaps the pretext to indict Mr. Taylor."

"Taylor often found comfort in rhetorical bouts to bolster his image locally as a no-nonsense leader, while ignoring the consequences such condescending remarks could have on Liberia's foreign relations."

"Power assets determine nations' position in the international arena. Liberia, like most underdeveloped countries is marginal in the circle of international power wielding and dealing; Taylor ignored this fact of foreign relations.

■ Max *Willie*

To

To Tina, Boto, Sabigi and Malcolm Max;
Diamond, Jasmyne, Xandel and Gabriel

To

Theo Dekonty Joseph who is an inexhaustible source
of support for the family

George Y. Tobey's Christianity, open-handedness, and humility

Jerry Verdier, a man whose generosity and humanity is unmatched
Among Liberian populations in the United States

And to my fight-back in the United States

ACKNOWLEDGEMENT

The initial draft of this manuscript inspired several of my friends particularly, Isaac Davies and Eli Barrolle who in turn encouraged me to write this book. Eric Mark, Esq. of the Eric M. Mark Law of New Jersey reviewed the draft of the manuscript to ensure there is no legal implication. I owe them all a debt of gratitude.

DEFINITIONS

Americo-Liberians: *the name given to a group of ex-slaves who migrated from the United States and made home in Liberia; their descendents*

Carte blanche: *complete freedom; free lead*

Custom-built: *specially made; commissioned*

ECOMOG: *ECOWAS Monitoring Group*

ECOWAS: *Economic Community of West African States; this West African regional organization intervened militarily in Liberia's 14-year civil strife*

Émigré: *an emigrant; an exile*

Equanimity: *level-headedness; calmness*

Fortress: *stronghold*

Gbarnga – *capital city of the most central Liberian county of Bong*

Gio and Mano: *the two major tribes of Nimba County*

Greater Liberia: *name given for 99% of Liberian territory administered by Charles Taylor during Liberia's civil war*

Indigenous: *native; original; aboriginal*

LDF: *Lofa Defense Force; one of several warring factions that participated in Liberia's 14 years of war. The LDF was a rival before becoming an ally of Charles Taylor's NPFL*

LURD: *Liberians United for Reconstruction and Development, a rebel group that invaded Liberia from Guinea two months into Charles Taylor's presidency*

Nimba: *One of 15 political sub-divisions (counties) of Liberia. Nimba is located in Northern Liberia.*

Nimbaian: *a native of Nimba County*

NPFL: *National Patriotic Front of Liberia; Charles Taylor-led organization that staged a revolt to dethrone Liberian dictator Samuel Doe*

NSA – *National Security Agency, Liberia's comparable to US Federal Bureau of Investigation, the FBI*

OAU: *Organization of African Unity, Africa's alike of EU (European Union); the OAU is now transformed to AU (African Union)*

Peripheral nations: *countries that are considered nonessential in the arena of international political dealing*

Proclivity: *liking; tasting; flavoring; tendency*

Raison d'être: *underlying principle; justification; basis*

Rife: *prevalent; widespread; endemic*

RUF: *Revolutionary United Front, a rebel group established in the 1990s in Sierra Leone by Foday Sankor to remove the Sierra Leonean regime from power*

SSS: *Special Security Service; the SSS is assigned to Liberia's Presidency*

ULAA: *Union of Liberian Associations in the Americas, an umbrella group of Liberians in the United States and other parts of North America*

ULIMO: *United Liberation Movement for Democracy, an arch rival of the NPFL during the Liberian civil war; ULIMO was led by media executive Alhaji Kromah and Roosevelt Johnson, a Liberian entrepreneur*

FOREWORD

When Charles Taylor called for the extinction of dictatorship in West Africa, Taylor became a symbol to many countries across the continent raising voice against tyranny. For more than a decade and half, Taylor altered the track of political events in Africa. Before his revolt against Samuel Doe was over in Liberia, there was fewer regimes left of autocracy in Africa; not without saying Taylor was a contradiction in disguise. He was a dictator himself.

Charles Taylor had a mixed-bag personality. Probably unlike other analysts, the author saw him through duo lens. Taylor had humanity. He was a great operative. His intelligence and knowledge of things was amazing. He demonstrated lucidity and great speech power. Taylor exercised immeasurable savvy in his dealings.

Then again, Charles Taylor was Machiavellian, a 'snake in the green grass'. He would smolder and scotch anything crossing the path of his power. He was cocky and arrogant, yet the degree of naivety he showed over and again in dealing with matters of far-reaching consequence was a flight of the imagination.

Taylor's "jail break" in the US in September 1985 to return to Liberia was thought to be a generation call to champion the foundation of resolving the many contradictions and challenges pervading the country for more than a century and half; the Samuel Doe era perhaps the zenith of dictatorial pandemic in Liberia.

However, after years of excruciating struggle against Samuel Doe's military regime, and up against the military might of 10 African nations, allied with four Liberian warring groups; having survived all, Taylor saw the country he set out to "liberate" a private design where everything within the border of Liberia belonged to him or under his control. The challenges Liberia faced, the primary target of Taylor's rebellion against Samuel Doe was unattended. As a copycat during the Doe years, Charles Taylor's notoriety led to his unceremonious exit from power following eight years as a rebellion leader, plus six years of an embattled presidency.

The debate about Charles Taylor is thought provoking; Taylor's impact on Liberia, Sierra Leone and Africa at large are noteworthy, particularly to African history. The Taylor phenomenon is a story that never dies. It is a tale with stripes and fine linings. Many observers have attempted to tell it, but in dissimilar ways, each from an assorted point of view.

'WHERE CHARLES TAYLOR WENT WRONG' lays bare the issues and events that culminated in the downfall of a man who remarkably transfigured Liberia, Africa's oldest independent republic. The book brings into full light the peak of Taylor's missteps and failures in Liberia, as well as his ill-advised role in Sierra Leone, a country with common border and heritage; his inflammatory foreign policy toward not only the US and other Western powers, but to neighboring countries as well was the basis for his international isolation, the lack of donor support to his government, and his eventual demise.

Perhaps no other writing has brought to focus yet Charles Taylor's slip-ups, as does this copy. Historians, students of history and policy makers, as well as political observers everywhere may find this work an attention in their analyses of war, peace and governance, particularly in Africa; thus the imperative of this book.

■ *The Author*

INTRODUCTION

When it was apparent that Liberia, a small West African nation was slipping more and more into domineering rule under Samuel Doe, Charles Taylor stepped forward to launch a communal uprising in Liberia; a people's rebellion that later culminated in perhaps one among the most brutal civil wars Africa has ever known. The war lasted from December 1989 to August 2003; well over 150 thousand people were killed.

Liberia enjoys the honor as Africa's first independent republic. Never been colonized by any country, Liberia's independence was self-declared on July 26, 1847. Freed slaves from North America, having been denied civil and human rights, launched into finding a homeland now called Liberia. The country was founded on the credo of liberty, justice and equality, a nation conceived as a gesture for humanity. A significant part of its symbol and practice is modeled and influenced by American culture. English is widely spoken as the country's official language. Its capital city is named for James Monroe, the 5th president of the United States of America. Liberia's aborigines are from parts of North and Central Africa and far preceded the arrival of the former slaves.

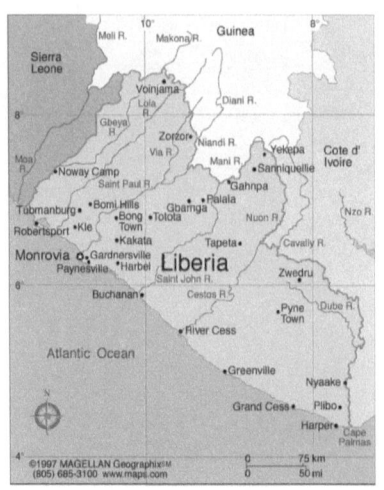

The country is situated on the West coast of Africa, flanked by Guinea to the North, Ivory Coast on the East, Sierra Leone on the West and the Atlantic Ocean to the South. It is a nation the size of Virginia in the U.S., and inhabited by three and a half million people.

During the long period that followed from 1847 to 1980, the ex-slaves, better known as Americo-Liberians exercised political and economic power exclusively in Liberia. The indigenous population was not included in the promise of freedom, political participation or justice. From its dawn in 1847 throughout its history Liberia has had astounding examples of unresponsive government.

The Liberian political system thus established remained under the firm grip of a select circle of immigrants and their descendents, from President Joseph Jenkins Roberts to President William Richard Tolbert. This, however was to change in 1980. An army sergeant named

Samuel Kanyon Doe intervened forcibly and took over state power at early dawn on April 12 of that year, the first full-fledged indigenous Liberian to head the country after nearly 140 years of Americo-Liberian rule. Doe was credited and supported initially by the majority of the population on the promise of political, social and economic reform. Samuel Doe ruled under military law until 1985 the year a new democratic constitution was to come into operation. However, the constitution was left largely unattended, let alone practiced. Doe,

Dictator Samuel Doe

banking on the loyalty and support of his clansmen, the Krahns to perpetuate his rule, viciously suppressed political opposition. Doe breached his promise to return to the barracks and to hand over powers to the civilians. He constituted a commission made up of loyalists and announced his candidacy for the presidential election that was to come in 1985. Doe clamped down on political opponents. However, Doe's unsavory reputation led to his dismal defeat at the polls, but he hijacked the election and converted the results as a win for himself. The entire Liberian population was distraught, so were many quarters of the international community. Dissent evolved steadily across the country. Doe used his military to suppress free speech and curtail rights and liberties. Human rights violations were pervasive, and the country was in a state of chaos. Most Liberians were of the opinion that Doe needed to step down. *Yet* scores of attempts, covert or overt to have Doe removed from power were violently crushed.

On December 24, 1989 Charles Taylor arrived on the scene; Taylor's entry into Liberia was out of the ordinary, given that he was in a maximum jail some more than 5,750 miles or 9,255 kilometers away in the United States. Taylor was being held at a Plymouth maximum prison in Boston, Massachusetts awaiting transportation back to Liberia to face embezzlement charges from Samuel Doe. Taylor "escaped" or "was let out of prison" and "commissioned" to lead a civilian armed rebellion against Doe. A group of prominent Liberians some of whom at the time were residents of the United States; Byron Tarr, Taylor E. Major, Clarence Simpson, Jr., Tom Woewiyou and others led openly by Liberia's 22nd

Tom Jucontoe Woewiyou

President Ellen Johnson-Sirleaf organized and gave support to Charles Taylor and his leadership of the Revolt in Liberia against Samuel Doe.

Ellen Johnson-Sirleaf

Taylor launched a communal uprising in Liberia that culminated in a brutal civil war, lasting from 1989 to 2003 with a momentous spillover effect on Africa, particularly on Sierra Leone, a country that shares common border and heritage with Liberia. Hundreds of thousands of people were killed in Liberia. A Sierra Leonean Special Court backed by the United Nations indicted Taylor, not for war excess in Liberia, but for his role in Sierra Leone's civil war. Taylor has since been condemned and committed to 50 years in jail.

THE ARGUMENT

Two competing perspectives emerged all at once when the UN-backed Sierra Leonean Special Court indicted Taylor on June 4, 2003 for 'war crimes and crimes against humanity'. Charles Taylor's devotees and sympathizers argue time and again that certain powerful nations and actors who held a less kind view of Taylor had all along plotted to see him put away indefinitely; that the opportunity to do so came coincidently through the Sierra Leonean Court. In other words, Charles Taylor was an object and now a victim of grand international conspiracy.

On the other hand, foes and detractors of Taylor have consistently rebuffed this hypothesis. They hold the view that the judgment meted out to Mr. Taylor is well proportioned and justified. They maintain that Taylor's actions or omissions are the leading factors to self-destruction. Both theories confirm the author's judgment, but more so, the latter, for the sake of the argument presented in this book.

The argument the author makes is not meant to challenge the raison d'être of Taylor's civilian armed rebellion, nor to query his wisdom for going into Sierra Leone, and unquestionably not to doubt the integrity of the UN-backed Court on its verdict to 'terminate' Taylor (considering Taylor's current age and the number of years he is subject to stay in jail). Not to argue also whether or not Taylor's indictment was motivated politically or was based solely on legal precedent. Issues surrounding the frantic international efforts to prosecute Charles Taylor for a war in Sierra Leone without regard for a consequential civil war conducted in Liberia by Taylor are left for a more conscientious and worthy debate.

In this work the author points out what he saw as the loads of mistakes or missteps that typified Taylor's war command and his six-year beleaguered presidency. While an émigré in Nigeria in 2003 Taylor told a close confidant he would "do it differently" if he had a second chance.

Throughout his service with the media particularly from 1990 to 2003 for the duration of Taylor's regimes, both armed and civilian, the author had come to know Mr. Taylor as a steady, impressive, charismatic leader, yet a lousy politician and statesman. The author was an associate of Taylor's, certainly not based on equal measurement of the scope of power or influence; but on wits, owing to mutual respect on views exchanged often behind close doors with Mr. Taylor on substantive issues. Some of the sessions were without disagreements.

One such instance of divergence with Taylor was sometime in April of 1996 when Monrovia, the capital city was engulfed by deadly renewed factional fighting. Taylor's men, dubbed as government forces had burgled a set of broadcast equipment belonging to a local Catholic radio station and reported the bounty to Mr. Taylor. Taylor summoned this author, who was at the time manager of Taylor's personal radio station to display the equipment and to instruct the author to take over and have the gadget installed for the use of the station. The author suggested otherwise having the equipment returned to the Catholic Church, and that that would be bad public relations if Mr. Taylor were to commandeer and take ownership of such private property. Yet on Mr. Taylor's insistence the gadget was mounted but briefly at Taylor's private station. The equipment was returned ultimately to the Catholic Mission on insistence of the author. The author was a participant-observer of Taylor at war and Taylor in the Executive Mansion. He was not an official in Taylor's administration.

TAYLOR'S SUPPOSED MISSION

Liberia had a rude awakening, and the entire West Africa region was shaken on December 24, 1989 when Charles Taylor started a rebellion against Samuel Doe. Commoners on the streets of African capitals commemorated Taylor's insurgency against Samuel Doe's regime as a model to rid West Africa of dictatorship. Quite the opposite, state houses across the Continent were of the opinion that the Charles Taylor-led people's uprising against a military dictator was a recipe that other civilian groups in Africa could follow to depose their leaders. A similar view was expressed in Karl P. Magyar's work 'Lessons for Peace-keeping, ECOMOG in Liberia' that "a successful ethnic-based overthrow of President Samuel Doe could have set the example for ethnic groups in Nigeria and other West African states to imitate. The reality of this issue is more apparent when combined with the knowledge that Nigerian dissidents were known to have trained in Libya and joined Taylor's forces in Liberia." In other words, the entire West Africa establishment feared the Taylor "virus" could spread to their countries if Taylor succeeded in toppling Samuel Doe militarily.

West Africa had the single largest concentration of dictators between 1980 and 1990 than any other region of the globe: Samuel Doe in Liberia, Ibrahim Banbagida and Sonii Abacha in Nigeria; Siaka Stevens and Joseph Momo in Sierra Leone, Sekou Toure and Lasannah Conte in Guinea, Gnassigbe Eyadema in Togo, and Sir Dauda Jawara in the Gambia. Others are Thomas Sankara and Blaise Comparorie in Burkina Faso, John Jerry Rawlings in Ghana, Felix Houpuet Boigny in the Ivory Coast, Matthew Kereku in Benin, and the list stretches on. However it is beyond the imagination of many how Charles Taylor, the man who was arguably, but widely acclaimed as typical to the cause of ridding the African continent of dictatorships fumbled so miserably. Taylor himself evolved into a menacing dictator.

INITIAL UNITED STATES GOODWILL

When it became evident that Charles Taylor had significantly gained upper hand in Liberia's civil war, Taylor received an outpour of international goodwill and political support. Taylor had grown effective control of 99% of Liberia's territory. West African leaders, as well as Western leaders paid courtesy calls on Taylor in Greater Liberia, named thus to describe Taylor's huge administrative area in Liberia during the war. Former United States President Jimmy Carter visited Taylor in 1991 in Harbel where Firestone Rubber Plantation is situated. Harbel was one of Taylor's fortresses during the war. President Carter's visit to Taylor followed the visits of two high-level State Department officials. French businesses and companies from other Western countries prospected for or were engaged in capital ventures in Taylorland.

In May 1998, one year following Mr. Taylor's election as President, several American black leaders in the U.S. organized and hosted an all-Liberian conference in Chicago, Illinois, involving Taylor's government, members of Liberia's civil society, a select group from the Liberian press including the author, and Liberian residents of the United States. The Rev. Jesse Jackson, President of Rainbow Coalition organized the conference and was supported by then Assistant Secretary of State for African Affairs Susan Rice. Several black business leaders and politicians attended the conference. The meeting called on Taylor to promote an open and inclusive social order in Liberia, and to respect the rights of the population. The conference organizers saw Charles Taylor then as one who could lead the West African sub-region into an epoch of bourgeoning democracy. Taylor's promise of departure from the past to a new era of good governance assured the conferees and U.S. officials that Liberia was up to becoming exemplary of democratic system in Africa.

CHARLES TAYLOR IN LIBERIA

One can safely surmise that the overwhelming view amid Liberian and many outside groups against Charles Taylor is not about his armed uprising per se, it was more about the way he executed the war. Majority of Liberians agreed then that the authoritarian regime of Samuel Doe where rights and liberties were being truncated must be called to account by any means necessary. On that basis, Taylor and the NPFL accrued massive support of the population and received their head-nod.

The truism that there can be no revolution (or any war for that matter) without blood shed is manifest in preceding wars everywhere. Whether it was World Wars I and II, American Revolutionary War, French Revolution, Chinese Revolution, Vietnam, Iraq, or the American Civil War; these all had chaos's and excesses. But the extent of the surpluses suffered in Liberia, a tiny country of three million and a half people, far surpassed what can be endured even by bare minimum human modesty.

When the author queried Taylor about the overkill of the operation, and why there wasn't order or control in the field, Taylor said two things: first, that passing out arbitrary orders of capital punishment for evil doers would pose a danger to his own (Taylor's) physical survival thus put at risk the entire objective and success of the Uprising. The fear was (in paraphrase), that any random execution of field commanders who were mostly Nimbaians responsible for these excesses, would be interpreted as Taylor getting rid of Gio and Mano people, and would have certainly produced a counter-upheaval. Second, the absence of order and control, as well as a chain of command, which Mr. Taylor called "zigzag structure" of the NPFL, was an imperative feature whereby the NPFL found its strength. Mr. Taylor said, "Our supremacy rests in our disorganization."

Out of the political process that ensued after eight years of a vicious civil war, Charles Taylor emerged as President of Liberia. The author views Taylor's election to the Presidency mainly on three accounts: (1) A notable segment of the population who harbored suspicion that the ECOWAS mission was in Liberia to obstruct Taylor's chances of becoming president, sympathized with Taylor and gave him their support, (2) the long and escalated military operation of ECOMOG against Taylor's NPFL without defeating Taylor, was perceived as putting the man in a position of military and political strength, and (3) significant support for Taylor's bid for president was based on anxiety; that a Taylor loss of election was the same as going back to war.

Charles Taylor was overwhelmingly elected President on July 19, 1997 in a contest that fielded 13 political parties. He was inaugurated in August of that year.

Taylor's first move was to set up a government of inclusion to which he made prominent appointment of his political and warring rivals, a move considered by some as superfluous, while others thought it was an ingenious decision. Liberians' hopes were ignited further, those who recognized Taylor as having the wherewithal, as well as the political poise and equanimity to dig the country out of brokenness and impoverishment.

Barely sixty days into Taylor's Presidency a fresh-armed incursion gripped the country that October from neighboring Guinea. The LURD rebel armed attack into Liberia became a pretext for the new Administration to defer nation building and divert "all resources to repel the war". It made good impression, but the explanation did not meet the kind judgment of unsuspecting citizens. In the face of the LURD attack, Taylor's circle of friends and associates were indulged in spectacle and self-aggrandizement while the rest of the population lived in dearth and was nibbling at whatever they could find.

TAYLOR'S DOMESTIC MISTAKES

Taylor's popularity began to wane before he had served a full one-year in office. The doubt about Taylor was mainly rooted in what the author considers more his mistakes rather than his failures on many fronts of governance, including administration, rule of law, rights of people and social service. Crime and illegal activities were a subset of evils that pervaded communities across the country.

Although Taylor gained much acclaim for stopping armed robbery, his first major mistake came earlier than later. In 1997, the same year of Taylor's installation as President, Sam Dokie, a renowned Liberian politician along with his wife and couple of his relatives was butchered and remains burned to ashes near the town of Palala off Gbarnga's highway. During the war, Dokie was a comrade of Taylor before joining forces with other warring factions against Taylor and the NPFL. The mystery that accompanied the death of Dokie was never addressed, let alone unraveled. Observers and other analysts placed the blame of the deaths squarely between the Police precinct in Gbarnga City, NSA in Monrovia and the hierarchy of the SSS at Taylor's Executive Mansion. Meanwhile Taylor condemned the murder and promised "a full investigation", a promise that was left to be fulfilled up to his dismissal from power in 2003. Taylor's failure to deal with such an issue of national consequence was the beginning of trouble in his presidency.

In 1999, Police Director Joe Tate, a police inspector and two other officers and a pilot died a horrible death when the Cessna plane they were traveling in from Buchanan crashed off the Roberts field highway. The plane was dissuaded landing at Roberts field for 'lack of lights' and instead directed to land in Monrovia. When the plane circled Monrovia for a considerable time period and could not touch down also because of shortage of lights, controls at Roberts field reported that lights had been restored and radioed the plane to return; on its way back, the plane apparently lost fuel or developed technical fault leading to its crash. The entire country was in condolence over the tragedy. Taylor promised the nation a thorough investigation of the matter and said he would publish its result. Taylor did not fulfill the promise.

Francois Massaquoi was an excellent sports administrator. He merged his Lofa Defense Force with Charles Taylor's NPFL at the near close of the civil war and became a friend of Taylor's. Massaquoi was one of several former rivals Taylor appointed to his post-war government, Massaquoi to the post of Minister of Youth and Sports. In the Taylor regime, Massaquoi was more than just a Minister; he was a logistician for the field command of Taylor in defense against the renewed war launched by LURD. Massaquoi was shot and killed on April 16, 2001 inside a helicopter about to land with supplies for Taylor's forces at a battlefront in Lofa County, a northern province of Liberia. The ground was supposed to be a friendly terrain. Massaquoi's killing left more questions than answers; however up to the time of Taylor's departure from Liberia, there was no appearance of activity to suggest that Taylor's assurance of an inquiry into the killing was genuine or sincere.

Taylor's unwillingness, more so his failure to restrain or punish unlawful behaviors within his armed forces and his Administration was considered a lack of moral compass or credibility to uphold the principle of the rule of law. Taylor adopted a way-out approach to governance, often applying the old NPFL zigzag model in conducting the affairs of state. In doing so, Mr. Taylor sometimes undermined the integrity of the government by making heads of Agencies or Ministries secondary to their subordinates, assigning duties to Assistants and Deputies; responsibilities, that are normally allocated for the Ministers by statutory mandate.

Taylor is Western-educated, knowledgeable in changing world processes, information and technology, as well as modern statecraft; one would believe that Taylor would have exploited this benefit in conducting the affairs of the government in an unadventurous way. To the contrary, Mr. Taylor relished the idea of a primordial town chieftaincy system where the country was perceived as a private enterprise. Taylor personalized a significant portion of the country's national resources to the benefit of friends and associates, and sometimes for political favors. He did not support a check and balance system. Accountability was often not evident.

CHARLES TAYLOR IN SIERRA LEONE

Taylor's involvement in Sierra Leone is not without precedent. Nations have stepped forward usually to support one of competing warring factions in countries nearest their borders or where their national interests are in jeopardy. For instance, the US intervened in Nicaragua in the 1980's on the side of the Contra rebels fighting the Nicaraguan government, a government the US detested. In December 1989 United States got involved in the crisis in Panama to "safeguard its interests and protect the lives of its citizens" there. In 1992-1994 the US went into Somalia and shifted the focus of the conflict to a contest between it and a faction, a move that suggested America's intention to re-assert itself in Somali politics (in Prof. George Klay Kieh's *International Organization and Peacekeeping in Africa, ECOMOG in Liberia' 1998 USA*). Nigeria mediated in the Chadian conflict in 1980 as peacekeepers under the OUA. The Force was seen as assuming increasing role of helping the government in power to repel advances made by one of the warring factions. The latest example of such foreign intervention was in 1990-2003 in Liberia where forces from more than 10 African nations participated. The African forces, led openly by Nigeria and loosely allied with ULIMO and other anti-Taylor factions had undertaken to prevent Taylor coming to power in Monrovia, and in doing so brought into question the neutrality status of the peacekeepers not from Taylor only, but from the United States as well *(*Max Willie's *The Social and Political Impact of the ECOWAS Intervention in Liberia'*, A Thesis, University of Liberia Library 1999 MONROVIA*)*. In these intervention efforts the idea was to ensure that warring contenders in countries of interest to these powerful nations do not replace friendly forces. Even so, in going into Sierra Leone, Charles Taylor ignored several key political realties: *First*, Liberia's power assets, hard or soft, were non-apparent at the time, including its commerce, trade and other economic indicators;

Foreign relations as well; the population was unsettled, there was a notable absence of a national military force, infrastructure remained broken, and Liberia also was in war and needed all available resources to reconstitute it. *In the second instance*, Taylor did not have the mandate to pursue such an aggressive foreign policy on behalf of Liberia. At the time, he was not an elected President. And *third*, Taylor should have disengaged Foday Sankor, the chief Sierra Leone rebel leader and should have promptly severed all support, financial, material or otherwise when the war in Sierra Leone reached the state of serious and lasting distress and affliction, and especially when local and international opinion was ingenuously unfavorable to the proclivity, particularly the shade or temper of the war. In other words, Taylor should have conceded on grounds that greater and lasting interests always trump personal friendships. That meant also that the International Community's prescription on Sierra Leone, one that included the isolation of Sankor, the rebellion leader should have been adopted in the pursuit in Sierra Leone of the foreign policy objective of Mr. Taylor.

With these blunders, plus his incessant support to Sankor in spite of objections from many quarters of the global community, Taylor became the main article of suspicion and was counted as the chief architect behind a war of such magnitude and grave consequence. This scenario, "international bias" aside, offered global actors the carte blanche or perhaps the pretext to indict Mr. Taylor.

CHARLES TAYLOR'S MISSTEPS IN FOREIGN RELATIONS & DIPLOMACY

Charles Taylor held a firm suspicion that powerful nations, particularly the United States have imposed their will and violated Liberia throughout history; 'it was time to put an end to this aggression'. Taylor overly used the word *sovereignty* to project a view of him as a leader of divine intervention; he depicted himself custom-built to curtail, if not to ground United States political influence in Liberia ad infinitum.

As discussed earlier, power assets determine nations' positions in the international arena. Liberia, like most underdeveloped countries is marginal in the circle of international power wielding and dealing, for this reason, the foreign policy objectives of these peripheral nations are usually at the mercy of great powers. Taylor ignored this fact of foreign relations. His consistent batter on the United States and other Western powers soon spelled trouble in his international relations.

On July 7, 1999 President Bill Clinton appointed Bismarck Myrick to serve as US Ambassador to Liberia. Myrick was the first African-American to be selected to serve in post-war Liberia. He took up assignment two years following Taylor's election. It was often rumored Myrick is a kin of Liberia's first president Joseph Jenkins Roberts. Both men are natives of Virginia in the US. Myrick's appointment to Liberia was reported to have strategic benefit to US and Liberia. He was to mend Liberian distrust of the United States on the basis of US indifference shown to the suffering endured by Liberians during 15 years of brutal civil war. Myrick was to press his country to lead Liberia's recovery efforts. Like one-time Ambassador William Swing, Mr. Myrick traveled Liberia's towns and villages extensively. However, the early good relationship between Myrick and President Taylor was soon to become astringent.

When the head of Taylor's ruling party called Ambassador Myrick "picky-hair", and that the Ambassador" could risk having his "a – " dragged in the streets of Monrovia", Taylor's silence was deafening, an indication of acquiescence. And the U.S. Embassy took it unkindly.

Furthermore, Charles Taylor's own rhetoric about the U.S. raised American suspicion of him and his government. At a live press conference sometime in 1998, Mr. Taylor lambasted the US for what he called America's steady history of dictating to Liberia, and that the days when Washington called to instruct Monrovia were long gone. Taylor often found comfort in these rhetorical bouts to bolster his image locally as a no-nonsense leader, while ignoring the consequences such condescending remarks could bear on Liberia's foreign relations.

When Osama Ben Laden masterminded the plane bombing of the World Trade Center in New York on September 11, 2001 killing two thousand 885 people, Taylor found a wide opening to mend barrier with the United States. He denounced the attacks and collaborated with the Americans in placing and maintaining rigorous security checkpoints around and within the vicinity of the US Embassy in Monrovia. The renewed friendship was short-lived, however. When U.S. double-downed on its call on Taylor to quit support to Foday Sankor's RUF in Sierra Leone, Taylor did not budge. The U.S. sent its diplomatic ombudsman Thomas Pickering to meet with Taylor in Monrovia. The encounter between the two men was everything but genial. Mr. Taylor cited time and again the principle of sovereignty, and continued in Sierra Leone, disregarding international condemnation.

SUMMARY & ANALYSIS

Charles Taylor's fate in Liberia is an invention of his actions, and certainly his avoidance to treat some things judiciously; not to say the UN-backed Court of Sierra Leone showed rectitude or was justified in condemnatory of Taylor's role in Sierra Leone's civil war, while ignoring the bigger and more devastating war prosecuted in Liberia by Taylor.

Taylor's blind-eye shown to the basic social needs of the population, plus his implicit support of a culture of impunity in Liberia invited public dissension. His failure to accomplish a major domestic goal de-legitimized his government. His missteps in foreign affairs and diplomacy produced solemn consequences; flaws in dealing with the United States, apart from the arrogance with which Taylor conducted himself in the arena of foreign relations were manifest time and again. Because of these defects, Taylor suffered consequences of immeasurable proportion.

- Western countries whose pledge of support Charles Taylor enjoyed as President of Liberia pulled back significantly in consideration of Taylor's domestic and foreign policies.
- Taylor's friendship with Taiwan at the expense of relations with Mainland China made his foreign policy goal more precarious.
- His daring stance on Sierra Leone in the face of international opposition made him an open target for isolation.
- Taylor's humiliating utterances about the US prompted Washington's disdain of his government. The US placed a ban on Taylor, his relatives, friends and associates to travel to United States, and by extension, persuaded her allies to hold back on assistance in response also to Taylor's rash foreign and domestic policies.
- Taylor's appointment of junior and sometimes second-rate officers to serve as heads of mission in major world capitals, demonstrated his contempt for those countries. These nations responded unreservedly and accordingly.
- At home, Taylor's legitimacy eroded steadily. Dissent became widespread, and armed rebellious activities flourished across most of the country.
- Taylor was forced into relinquishing power and cast into exile.

However his lack of discretion in the administration of Liberia, and his multiple blunders committed in foreign relations; if anyone were to ask whether this is good reason enough to drag Charles Taylor to the International Court of Justice in The Hague and condemn him to life in jail, my answer would be HELL NO! Should Taylor bear significant burden for his actions or lapses in Liberia? WITHOUT A DOUBT!

A PROFILE OF CHARLES TAYLOR

Charles Ghankay Taylor is the 21st President of the Republic of Liberia. He is the son of an Americo-Liberian man and a woman of the Gola tribe of Liberia. Taylor was born on January 28, 1948 in Arthington, a township on the outskirt of Monrovia, the capital city. Born Charles McArthur Taylor, he adopted 'Ghankay' (a Gola tribal forename) as his middle name to rally solidarity and support of the indigenous population during his years at war and as president of Liberia. Taylor attended Kakata Rural Teachers Training Institute in Kakata, Margibi County and University of Liberia before moving to the United States for further study. In the US Taylor attended Bentley College in Waltham, Massachusetts where he earned a Bachelor of Arts degree in Economics in 1977. Taylor was National Chairman of the Board of ULAA. He became a vocal opponent of former Liberian President William R. Tolbert. Taylor ironically returned to Liberia briefly on invitation from President Tolbert. When Tolbert was assassinated in a coup d'état orchestrated by Samuel Doe in April 1980 Taylor returned to Liberia permanently and took up a position in Doe's military government as Director-General of General Services Agency. In May 1983 Doe replaced Taylor as head of the Agency and accused him of misusing nearly one million dollars. Taylor absconded to the US where he was arrested and detained two years after, awaiting to be transported back to Liberia to face charges of misappropriation. In September 1985 Taylor 'broke jail' and removed himself from the United States back to Africa where he built an army of Liberian refugees. In December 1989 Taylor and the NPFL entered Liberia; and the country broke loose into successive battles with Samuel Doe's military.

After series of local and international peace initiatives, agreement was concluded in 1995. In 1997 Taylor became President of Liberia in an election he won hands down, election local and international observers acclaimed as free, fair and transparent. During his tenure as President, Taylor battled outside armed incursion, and encountered harsh criticisms over his domestic and foreign policies.

In June 2003 Taylor was charged on 11 counts of war crime and crime against humanity. He was forced into resignation. On August 11, 2003 Taylor stepped down from office and went into exile in Nigeria. However the UN/Sierra Leonean Court pressed charges of war crimes against the former Liberian President. Taylor's trial in The Hague in The Netherlands began on June 4, 2007 and continued for nearly six years before he was found guilty in April 2012. Taylor has been in jail since to serve 50 years.